Richa Yamini Goel

Quick Reference Guide (QRG)

for

Risk Management

2 | Quick Reference Guide — Risk Management

Richa Yamini Goel

Richa Yamini Goel

Preface

This book is going to help you understand the basic concept of Risk Management in reference to standards, ISO 31001:2018 and ISO 27001:2013 which are a published standard from ISO. We have tried to gather the information from various sources and providing the same at a single place to be ready to help you understand the concept of Risk Management which is now an integral part of all the new standards including, ISO 9001:2015 (quality Management System), ISO 14001:2015 (Environmental Management System), ISO 27001:2013 (Information Security Management System).

In this book, we are trying to put the information from various references and rephrase the same in simple language for easy understanding. The purpose and focus of this book is the concept of Risk Management with respect to Data Security.

Disclaimer: This book is not a replacement for the internal/ external auditor trainings, or awareness session. This is just a handy booklet for quick reference.

4 | Quick Reference Guide — Risk Management

Richa Yamini Goel

Richa Yamini Goel

Contents

6 | Quick Reference Guide – Risk Management

Richa Yamini Goel

Richa Yamini Goel

Risk Management - Introduction

Risk is a scenario where there is a possibility of events or activities hindering the achievement of an organization's strategic and operational objectives. The risk is the existence of vulnerability which can later expand to become a failure of the process. Discovering vulnerabilities is important, but being able to estimate the associated risk to the business is just as crucial. For this purpose, Risk Management comes into the picture.

Risks are unfavorable events happening to the organization or other stakeholders. Control can give the required protection from risk. Risk identification and assessment are essential for the organization so that they can plan for the controls accordingly.

Risk Management is a preventive approach to forecast and handle unexpected events which can result in major failures and/ or blockers to the normal process of business operations. These risks need to be identified, analyzed, evaluated and treated using appropriate controls.

We can also say that risk management is the process of identifying, assessing and controlling threats to an organization's capital, reputation, operations, and earnings. These threats, or risks, could originate from a

Richa Yamini Goel

wide variety of planned and unplanned sources, including financial uncertainty, legal liabilities, strategic management errors, accidents, and/ or natural disasters.

According to ISO 31000, the risk is defined as the "effect of uncertainty on objectives" and an effect, in this regard, can be a positive or negative deviation from what is expected.

When we talk about risks, Organizations of all types and sizes face external and internal factors and influences that make it unclear whether they will achieve their objectives. These factors and influences can originate from the risks. Hence, we need to consider these factors to identify the risks to the Organization.

Once the Risks are identified, they need to be assessed, evaluated and then treated appropriately. There are various methodologies available to implement this Risk Management process, although we are only going to discuss a few of them here.

The purpose of Risk Management is to identify risks and determine the probability of occurrence, the resulting impact, and additional safeguards that would mitigate this impact. Regardless of the prevention techniques employed, possible threats that could arise inside or outside the organization are assessed.

Richa Yamini Goel

Although the exact nature of potential disasters or their resulting consequences are difficult to determine, it is beneficial to perform a comprehensive risk assessment of all threats that can realistically occur to the organization

Richa Yamini Goel

Risk Management As A Process

An information security risk assessment is a formal, top management-driven process and sits at the core of an ISO 27001 information security management system (ISMS). Managing these risks is an iterative process and assists organizations in setting strategy, achieving objectives and making informed decisions. It is a part of governance and leadership and is fundamental to how the organization is managed at all levels. It contributes to the improvement of management systems.

Risk should be identified from all perspectives including all the interested parties. The Organization shall consider the external and internal context of the organization, including human behavior and cultural factors while identifying the risks.

Managing risk is based on the principles, framework, and process. These components might already exist in full or in part within the organization, however, they might need to be adapted or improved so that managing risk is efficient, effective and consistent.

The inputs to create a Risk Management sheet can be:

- Internal & External Issues of the Organization
- Security Incidents
- New Business Drivers
- Natural Calamities
- Organizational Objectives
- Professional Hazards
- Past Incidents
- Industrial Events
- Government Regulations
- Audits
- Bulletins and Forums

and many more.

The Risk Management, often known as Risk Analysis, is a complete process involving Risk Assessment and Treatment processes. The risk management process involves the basic 5 steps:

1. Establish a risk management framework
2. Identify risks
3. Analyze risks
4. Evaluate risks
5. Risk Treatment

Fig 2.1 Risk Management Process

Richa Yamini Goel

The main purpose of Risk Management is to find out which incidents could occur (i.e. assess the risks) and then to identify the most appropriate ways to avoid such incidents (i.e. treat the risks). After this, you also have to assess the importance of each risk so that you can focus on the most important ones.

Therefore, risk management is about decision making and taking actions to address uncertain outcomes, controlling how risks might impact the achievement of business goals.

We cannot access and control all the possible risks around the Organization, hence, we focus on the risks around the organisation's valuable information.

One size does not fit all and not all the risks are bad, the risks do create opportunities too, however, the most of the time it is threat-focused.

Risk is defined as the probability of an event and its consequences. A Risk management process focuses on identifying what could go wrong, evaluating which risks should be dealt with and implementing strategies to deal with those risks.

Richa Yamini Goel

Types of Risks

There are various ways to categorize the risks. These risks may originate due to the need for strategic decisions, requirements for compliance, implementation of certain operations, impacting the financial transactions, market competition and reputation of the Organization. In an Organization, the risks can revolve around:

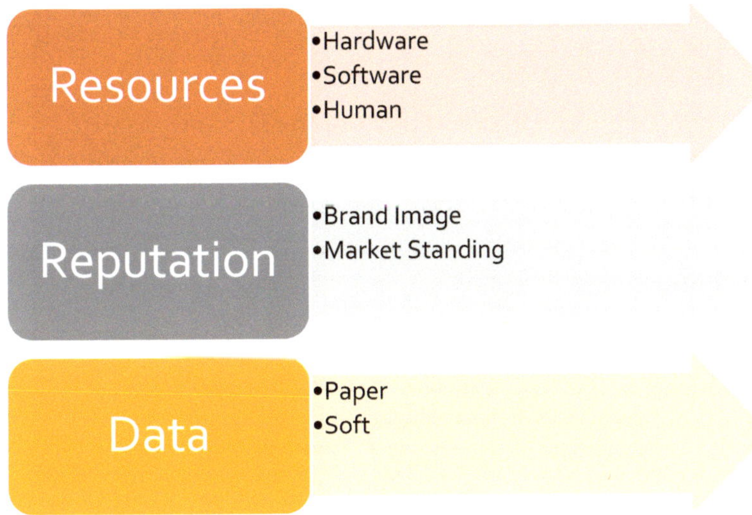

Fig 3.1 Types of Risks

We need to ensure that we can identify the critical elements that may get impacted due to the forecasted risks and the same can be treated by putting various controls in place to tackle the risks.

Richa Yamini Goel

The risks are identified under the recognized high-level categories. These risks are then accessed to understand the impact of the risk on the Organization.

The risk identification helps the Organization to be prepared for the impact these risks may counter. If the Organization is prepared with the controls which can be implemented to avoid or tackle these risks, the monetary and reputational loss can be controlled by 80%. Hence, it is really important to put in the appropriate controls.

With constant industrial and technological changes, it is also required to review these risks on a defined period. This opportunity helps the Organization to identify, filter, optimize, re-access and update the risks and their risk ratings.

Richa Yamini Goel

Risk Management Framework

The first step is to create ground rules for the complete Risk Management.

Every business faces risks that could present threats to its success.   You need to define rules on how you are going to perform risk management because you want your whole organization to do it with a clear intention and systematic way.   The biggest issues with the implementation of risk assessment are if different parts of the organization perform it in a different way.

Therefore, it is important to define whether you want qualitative or quantitative risk assessment, which scales you will use for qualitative assessment, what will be the acceptable level of risk, etc.

It is important to consider that the methodologies to identify for risk management should consider their alignment with Organizational objectives, security and quality objectives, and internal & external issues.

While creating a risk management framework, it is important to identify:

- the formats to be used,
- information to capture,
- the calculation methods,
- risk approving authority,
- members of the risk management committee and their roles and responsibilities,
- risk reviewing methodology and frequency
- communication methods
- actions for encountering any undocumented risks

For implementing the above, it is important to document the same in a controlled document, or procedure. A handy working document, like a risk register, can come as a savior.

A well documented process helps in better implementation and helps is handling uncertainties as you'll be better informed on the actions to take. If properly managed and maintained, it will also act as an insurance mechanism in the scenario where such an event is raised.

It is also important to map your risks with the three pillars:

- **Confidentiality:** information is not made available or disclosed to unauthorised individuals, entities or processes.

- **Integrity:** safeguarding the accuracy and completeness of information assets.

- **Availability:** being accessible and usable upon demand by an authorised entity.

A risk register can be maintained to keep a track of all the risks and their related analysis. The Risk Register is a confidential document and hence should have limited access. The accesses for the same need to be identified and documented.

Identifying & Analyzing Risks

The second step is to identify and analyze the risks in the system.

To help to identify the risks, it is important to understand the impact of these risks.   This is the process of examining each work area and work task for the purpose of identifying all the possible risks which are "inherent in the job".

The important points to consider when identifying risks are:

1. Let the organization employees, of all levels, identify the risks. If the identification of risks on trusts to top or middle management, we may not be able to identify certain crucial risks.
2. Do not restrict certain types of risks.   Let employees come with whatever they think is a risk, and later filter them as per need. This helps in opening new avenues.
3. Do not exclude internal or external risks. There may be directly or indirectly impacting the Organization's progress.

Richa Yamini Goel

4. Do not exclude risks by transferring the risks internally or externally without assessing them.
5. Encourage the employees to contribute by identifying more risks over time.

The identified risks by the employees, need to be filtered after discussing the impact of the risk management committee. The committee ensures which decisions need to be part of the final document depending upon the impact of the risks, in the case arises.

These identified risks need to be documented and approved by the top management.

Risk Identification is a crucial process and requires a lot of discussions. There are various tools which can be used to gather inputs for the identification of risks, like:

- Internal and external issues
- Security objectives
- Security Trends
- News and Bulletins

Risk assessment is carried out for all the Services and related assets that are identified for each process. Risk Owner is identified for each Risk, who is responsible to identify the risks and mitigation strategy with the Management. Management is authorized to accept the residual risks after reviewing the risk assessment with written approval.

Richa Yamini Goel

Threats considered for Risk Analysis

The following are the various threats that can be considered for the purpose of risk assessment. We have classified the threats into four categories as follows:

- ➢ **Natural threats**
  - Flooding
  - External Fire
  - Seismic Activity
  - Epidemic
  - Storms and Rains
- ➢ **Facility related threats**
  - Internal fire or explosion
  - Structure Collapse
  - Failure of detection system/alarm system, access control mechanism
  - Water Leakage
  - Power failure / Fluctuation
  - HVAC Failure
- ➢ **Human Related Threats**
  - Theft
  - Bomb Threat
  - Vandalism
  - Terrorism
  - Computer Crimes (Hacking, Intrusion, Denial of Service attacks, Leakage of information (electronic documents), Illegal use of Information Technology assets, Deletion of Sensitive documents, etc.,
  - Malicious Codes (Computer Viruses, network worms, Trojan horses)
  - Inappropriate media handling (Unauthorized disclosure of information asset, misuse of media)

Richa Yamini Goel

➤ **Technical Threats**
- System Hardware Failure
- Operating System failure
- Application software failure
- Data Corruption or loss of data
- System failure due to system acceptance / improper change
- Network failure
- Telecommunication Failure

Based on the type of services, the applicable threats are evaluated. While carrying out the risk assessment, the controls that are currently in place are analyzed and are measured for their effectiveness and efficiency. During the risk assessment process, any loopholes in the current controls are identified and steps are taken to improve upon.

Richa Yamini Goel

Accessing Risks

After identifying risks, it is very important to access those risks to calculate their impact on the Organizational processes and image. All the identified risks need to be assessed as per their impact levels. The impact levels may be identified as

- High, Medium, or Low, or
- Critical, Major, or minor, or
- Using numerical rating, or
- Any other methodology.

The risk impact can be calculated by identifying the level of loss the organization may suffer if the risk occurs. For e.g., if the risk identified is fire, the loss of assets and information within the organization may be high. These can be calculated with the help of identifying and accessing the vulnerabilities and threats.

Vulnerability

The various vulnerabilities that may exist in AMS Inform are identified. The presence of vulnerability may either increase the probability of occurrence of the threat or increases the impact of the threat.

Examples of vulnerabilities include (but not limited to):

Richa Yamini Goel

Threats	Vulnerability
System Hardware Failure	*• Hardware is not maintained properly* *• Temperature controls are not adequate*
Operating System failure	*• System parameters are not configured properly* *• Technical vulnerabilities exist*
Application software failure	*• Application software not configured adequately*
Data Corruption or loss of data	*• Backup process insufficient* *• Backup restoration not carried out*
Network failure	*• Redundant data card not available* *• No alternate network service provider*
External fire	*• No water outlets, surrounding the building* *• Inadequate space for the fire brigade to access the building*
Internal fire	*• Fire extinguisher not serviced adequately* *• No person is trained on using the fire extinguisher* *• Fire extinguisher is not available in the proper place* *• Fire alarm and smoke detector are not available* *• Inflammable materials are stored*
Seismic activity	*• The building is in earth quake prone area*

Richa Yamini Goel

Threats	**Vulnerability**
Structure Collapse	• *Proper maintenance is not carried out for building*
Flooding and Heavy Rain	• *Drainage ducts are blocked and hence flood waters are stagnated* • *Lightning arrester not functioning*
Water leakage/Plumbing problem	• *No maintenance activities carried out for the internal pipes*
Power failure/fluctuation	• *UPS is not maintained as per the requirement.* • *Diesel is not available for the generator*
Telecommunication failure (including PBX and Internet)	• No alternate service provider
Theft and unauthorized physical access *Vandalism, Terrorism and Bomb Threat*	• Inadequate physical security • Inadequate monitoring
Malicious codes	• Antivirus application is not updated with the latest signatures • Desktops not installed with the antivirus application
Computer crimes	• Firewall not configured as per the requirement • Access to systems not restricted

Richa Yamini Goel

Once all the risks are evaluated as per impact, they need to be assessed for the CIA - Confidentiality, Integrity, and Availability. Again, for each risk, the chances of breach of confidentiality, integrity, and availability of information saved within the Organizational scope need to calculated. That is, if a certain risk is encountered, how many levels of confidentiality, integrity, or/ and availability of the important information will be compromised.

Likelihood or Occurrences are evaluated for the purposes of the Security Risk Assessment which has to be the quantifiable probability of occurrence of a risk. A sample grid which can be used is as below:

Level	Rating	Explanation
1	Rare	Occurs only in exceptional circumstances
2	Unlikely	Could occur but not expected. Could occur "after several years"
3	Possible	Could occur "within a year or so"
4	Likely	Will probably occur in most circumstances. Could occur within "weeks to months"
5	Almost Certain	Is expected to occur in most circumstances. Could occur within "days to weeks"

There are various methodologies to access the risks, but here we will discuss only a few samples and simple methods.

Method 1:

1. Calculate the CIA values for each risk.
   a. For high confidentiality, the scale can be 5 and for low confidentiality, the scale can be 1

Richa Yamini Goel

b. For availability and integrity and scale should be 0 or 1, as it may be compromised or may not be compromised.

Fig 5.1 CIA Calculation

2. For each identified risk, calculate the likelihood of occurrence of each risk, on the basis of historical data. The same can be calculated on the scale of 1-5, where 1 is Low frequency and 5 is High frequency. (as X)

3. Calculate the impact of each risk if encountered on the scale of 1-5, where 1 is Low impact and 5 is High impact. (as Y)

4. Add the CIA values. (as Z)

5. Multiply X, Y and Z.

6. This will give you a risk score.

Richa Yamini Goel

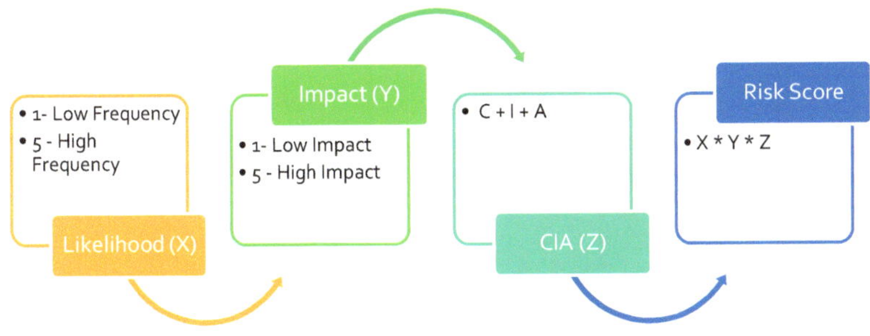

Fig 5.2 Risk Calculation : Method 1

Method 2:

1. Calculate the severity of each identified risk for the asset on the scale of 1-3, 1 being low and 3 being high, on the basis of Organizational loss.
2. Calculate the likelihood, depending upon the historical data on the scale of 1-3, 1 being lowest and 3 being highest.
3. Multiply Severity and Likelihood. (as X)
4. Calculate the CIA on High, Medium and Low. (High being 3, Medium as 2 and Low as 1)
5. Add the CIA values. (as Y)
6. Multiply X and Y values to get the risk score.

Richa Yamini Goel

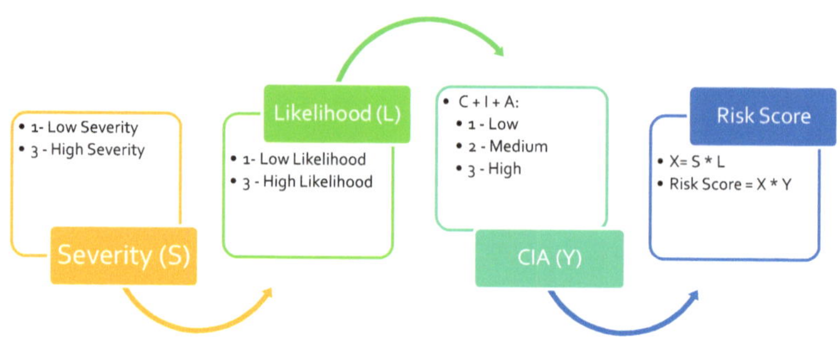

<u>Fig 5.3 Risk Calculation : Method 2</u>

These risk scores can then be used to measure the risks. The actions on the risks can be taken accordingly. The risk owner(s) need to be identified for each risk. These risk owners are responsible for ensuring to keep a check on these risks.

Alternate Method:

Another sample risk assessment section is given below:

Risk Action	Risk Validity	C/ A= Confidentiality/ Availability Rating	I = Integrity Rating	LR = Likelihood Rating	Risk Rating	
		Negligible - 1	No - 0	Rare - 1		
Avoid	A=Acceptable	Low - 2	Yes - 1	Unlikely - 2	Risk Value	Risk Rating
Accept	NA=Not acceptable	Medium - 3		Possible - 3	1 to 12	Low
Mitigate		High - 4		Likely - 4	13 to 28	Medium
Transfer		Extreme - 5		Almost Certain - 5	More than 28	High

<u>Fig 5.4 Risk Calculation : Matrix</u>

Richa Yamini Goel

After calculating the risk score by using either of the above methods or the combination of the same, a grid needs to be prepared to identify the types of risks on which the action can be taken. An example of the same is given below:

Impact / Probability	1	2	3	4	5	
1	1	2	3	4	5	A
2	2	4	6	8	10	A*
3	3	6	9	12	15	NA
4	4	8	12	16	20	
5	5	10	15	20	25	

Fig 5.5 Risk Score Grid

Richa Yamini Goel

Mitigating Risks

Once the risks are accessed, the same need to be mitigated by taking appropriate actions on each of the risks. There are majorly 4 types of actions which can be taken on any risk to control them:

1. **Accept Risk:** The stakeholders who are responsible for risk can choose to accept a risk.
2. **Mitigate Risk:** Actions are taken to reduce risk to an acceptable level.
3. **Avoiding Risk:** A risk may be avoided by implementing a work-around or providing a temporary solution.
4. **Transfer Risk:** A risk may be transferred to another organization or individual.

Risk Acceptance is the process of accepting the risks in case the risks cannot be mitigated, reduced, transferred or avoided. But to accept the risk, the approval from the top management and Information security team.

Risk Reduction/ Mitigation is the reduction of the risk score with the help of the implementation of controls on the risks, till the acceptable level. These controls are recorded, implemented and monitored.

Risk avoidance is the elimination of hazards, activities, and exposures that can negatively affect an organization's assets. Whereas risk management aims

Richa Yamini Goel

to control the damages and financial consequences of threatening events, risk avoidance seeks to avoid compromising events entirely.

Risk Transfer involves contractual obligations, where the third party takes the responsibility to control the risks of the Organization. This contract usually also covers the SLA (Service Level Agreements) and the penalties on not meeting these SLAs.

Accepting Risks

The risks are accepted with the approval of the top management.

Mitigating Risks

The risks are mitigated by taking appropriate measures to reduce the risks.

Avoiding Risks

The risks are avoided by providing a work around.

Transfer Risks

The risks are transferred to some third party.

Fig 6.1 Risk Mitigation

Richa Yamini Goel

The organization decides on the assurance required from the controls and countermeasures implemented to manage each risk and approve the acceptable level of risks. The criteria for accepting the risks shall depend on the balance between the costs of implementing the controls to reduce the risks against the benefit obtained from implementing the controls.

The risks identified as part of risk assessment exercise will be taken as an acceptable level of risk only if either of the following criteria is met:

1) The Information Security Committee perceives that the cost of control or effectively mitigating the risk is greater than the risk. E.g. Shifting an entire factory to a location that is less earthquake prone.
2) The risk is going to be nullified / mitigated in the near future due to changes in the control environment or operating environment.
3) Risks beyond the control of company management and are primarily of National / global nature
4) Implementation of control might create concerns regarding the safety of employees and/or humans in the neighborhood.
5) The control impedes the operations

Risks that have a "low" score on the risk level are accepted by the organization after considering the business exigencies. Risks that are in the "medium" and "high" range are carefully evaluated and based on business requirements and costs of controls, an organization can recommend its acceptance.

Richa Yamini Goel

Residual risks after implementing the proposed controls are also need to be accepted and approved by the management.

Richa Yamini Goel

Monitoring and Closing Risks

Once the risks are identified and analyzed, they need to be monitored regularly. The risks can be closed in due course of time if they are permanently eliminated from the system.

The review and monitoring of the risks need to be done at least once a year or on the defined frequency in the schedule to improve the business performance. Monitoring risks involves looking for identified, and residual risks, identifying any new risks, taking quick corrective action when a risk materializes, planning further preventive actions when you identify a trend of a new risk and measuring the effectiveness of risk responses, with the changing technology, legislation, and other controlled and uncontrolled factors.

While monitoring the risks, the risk score can be updated depending upon the change of factors, government policies, technological advancements, location, scope, opportunities, challenges and many others. Hence, it is important to revisit the Organizational risks after every major change.

The risks may get closed in certain scenarios. These identified risks can be closed only with the approval of the top management. Once a risk is closed, there is no need to revisit or review the closed risks in every scheduled frequency.

The risks can be closed in certain scenarios like:
- When the source of risk is eliminated.
- When the risk is not the part of the process anymore, due to changes in technology, policies or any other factor.
- When the risk is bypassed due to renovation/ location change.

In a similar kinds of scenarios, the identified risk can be closed and removed from the risk register.

References

ISMS Online. *ISMS Online.* [Online] https://www.isms.online/iso-27001/information-security-risk-management-explained/.

Risk Assessment Treatment Process. *Advisera.* [Online] https://advisera.com/27001academy/knowledgebase/iso-27001-risk-assessment-treatment-6-basic-steps/.

2016. Risk Management. *www.techtarget.com.* [Online] August 2016. https://searchcompliance.techtarget.com/definition/risk-management.

Standardization, International Organization of. 2018. *ISO 31000:2018.* s.l. : ISO, 2018.

About The Author

Richa Yamini Goel is a Certified Lead Auditor for ISO 9001:2015 and ISO 27001:2013. She has more than 20 years of industry experience and has been associated with multiple certification bodies for external and internal audits and imparting internal and lead auditor training on the ISO standards.   She also assists Organizations in the implementation of ISO guidelines and helps them in optimizing their processes.

She has written and published a few more books on Amazon on ISO.

For any queries/ feedback/ suggestions, you can directly contact her at richa@gyanedgeconsulting.com.

38 | Quick Reference Guide – Risk Management

Richa Yamini Goel